THE U.S. MARINE CORPS

★ INSIDE THE U.S. MILITARY ★

ROSEN PUBLISHING

BY TANNER BILLINGS

Library of Congress Cataloging-in-Publication Data

Names: Billings, Tanner, author.
Title: The U.S. Marine Corps / Tanner Billings.
Description: New York : Rosen Publishing, [2022] | Series: Inside the U.S. military | Includes bibliographical references and index. | Contents: Air, Ground, and Sea -- The Spirit of the Marines -- Marines at War -- Gear Up -- Famous Marines.
Identifiers: LCCN 2020005083 | ISBN 9781978518643 (library binding) | ISBN 9781978518636 (paperback) | ISBN 9781978518650 (ebook)
Subjects: LCSH: United States. Marine Corps--History--Juvenile literature.
Classification: LCC VE23 .B49 2022 | DDC 359.9/60973--dc23
LC record available at https://lccn.loc.gov/2020005083

Published in 2022 by The Rosen Publishing Group, Inc.
29 East 21st Street, New York, NY 10010

Designer: Sarah Liddell
Editor: Kate Mikoley

Photo credits: Cover, background used throughout Constantin Sellea/Shutterstock.com; p. 4 David H. Wells/Corbis Documentary/Getty Images; p. 5 Tyler Stableford/The Image Bank/Getty ImagesPlus/Getty Images; p. 7 dustin77a/Shutterstock.com; pp. 9, 31 Joe Raedle/Staff/Getty Images News/Getty Images; p. 11 Raymond Boyd/Contributor/Michael Ochs Archives/Getty Images; p. 13 David Hume Kennerly/Contributor/Hulton Archive/Getty Images; p. 15 BotMultiChillT/Wikimedia Commons; pp. 17, 33 Bettmann/Contributor/Bettmann/Getty Images; p. 20 FDRMRZUSA/Wikimedia Commons; p. 21 DOD/Handout/Getty Images Sport/Getty Images; p. 22 Mx. Granger/Wikimedia Commons; p. 24 (photo) Albinto/Wikimedia Commons; p. 24 (MARPAT) Doubleailes/Wikimedia Commons; p. 24 (old camo) RazorGraphix/Shutterstock.com; p. 25 Robert Nickelsberg/Contributor/Getty Images News/Getty Images; p. 27 Slick-o-bot/Wikimedia Commons; p. 30 Stocktrek Images/Stocktrek Images/Getty Images; p. 35 Drew Angerer/Staff/Getty Images News/Getty Images; p. 37 NASA/Handout/Hulton Archive/Getty Images; p. 42 Michael Kovac/Contributor/Getty Images Entertainment/Getty Images; p. 44 Scott Olson/Staff/Getty Images News/Getty Images; p. 45 U.S. Navy/Handout/Getty Images News/Getty Images.

Portions of this work were originally authored by Michael Portman and published as *Marine Corps.* All new material this edition authored by Tanner Billings.

Printed in the United States of America

Some of the images in this book illustrate individuals who are models. The depictions do not imply actual situations or events.

CPSIA compliance information: Batch #BSRYA22: For further information contact Rosen Publishing, New York, New York at 1-800-237-9932.

CONTENTS

Words in the glossary appear in **bold** type the first time they are used in the text.

AIR, GROUND, AND SEA

The different branches of the U.S. military often work together to ensure the safety and security of the country and its citizens. While each branch performs all sorts of duties, some of the forces are charged with protecting the country on certain **fronts**. For example, the navy mainly defends the country at sea, the air force does so in the air, and the army does so on land.

THE MARINE CORPS WAS FORMED IN 1775. IT HAS TAKEN PART IN EVERY WAR THE UNITED STATES HAS FOUGHT.

The Marine Corps, however, doesn't fit so cleanly into one of these categories. The corps is part of the Department of the Navy, but its members fight in the air, on the ground, and at sea.

CHAPTER ONE: THE SPIRIT OF THE MARINES

The purpose of the U.S. Marine Corps, also known simply as the marines, is to quickly respond to any threat the United States faces, anywhere in the world. The marines must always be ready for any mission. Since its formation, the marines have faced some of the biggest challenges in U.S. military history.

★ EXPLORE MORE ★

THE EAGLE, GLOBE, AND ANCHOR IS THE OFFICIAL EMBLEM OF THE MARINE CORPS. THE EAGLE REPRESENTS THE UNITED STATES, THE GLOBE REPRESENTS THE MARINES' WORLDWIDE PRESENCE AND COMMITMENT, AND THE ANCHOR REPRESENTS ITS CLOSE TIES AND HISTORY WITH THE NAVY.

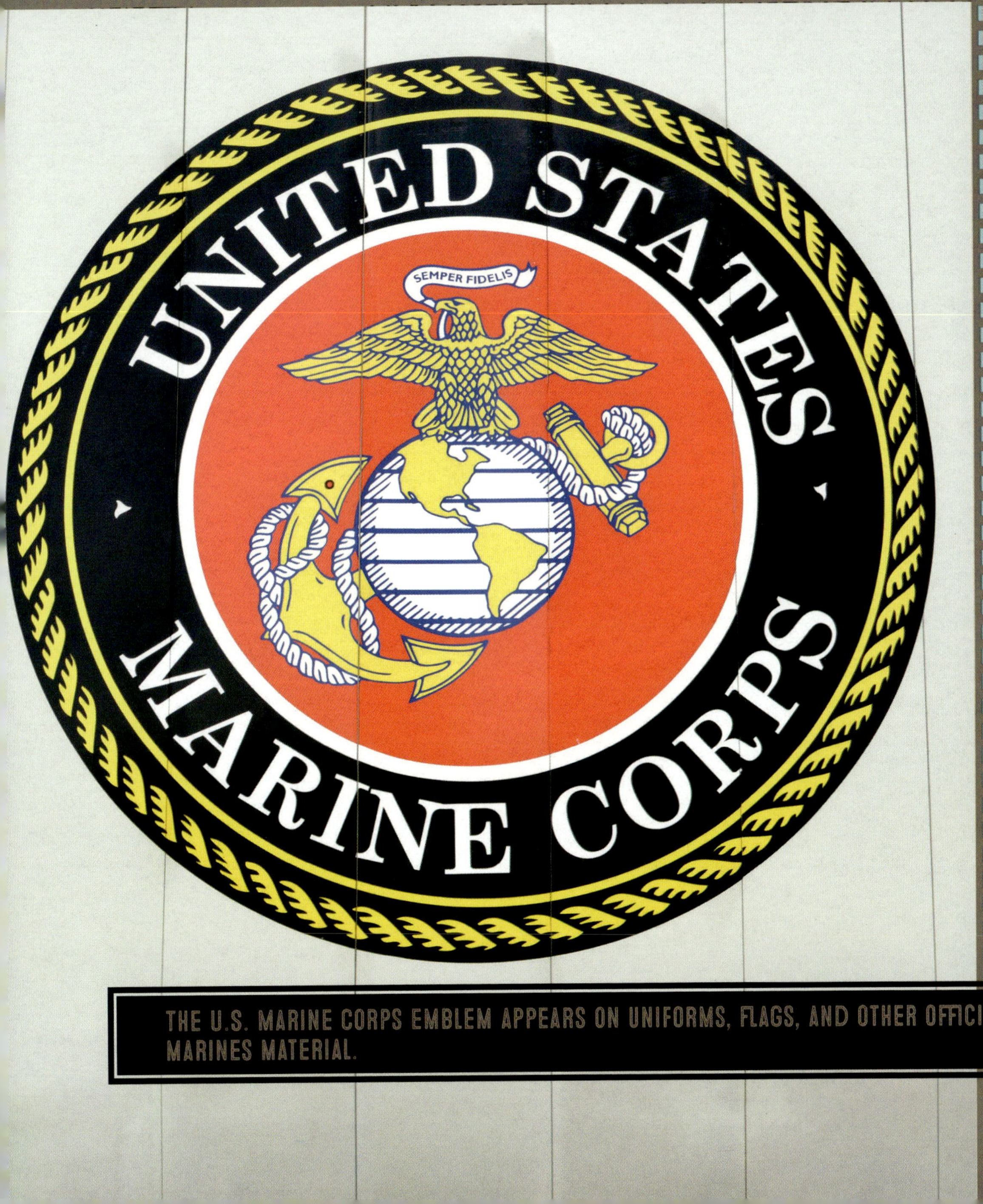

THE U.S. MARINE CORPS EMBLEM APPEARS ON UNIFORMS, FLAGS, AND OTHER OFFICIAL MARINES MATERIAL.

FORMING THE FORCE

The U.S. Marine Corps was founded on November 10, 1775. The Continental Marines were a naval infantry created to fight the British during the American Revolution. They provided security for naval vessels and led raids on British ships and forts. After the war, the Continental Marines came to an end. In 1798, the marines were brought back to protect U.S. ships from pirates near Africa. In 1805, the marines won the Battle of Derna in Tripoli, in what's now Libya. It was the first overseas land battle the United States fought and the first time the American flag was raised in another country.

INFANTRY: SOLDIERS TRAINED TO FIGHT ON FOOT

RAID: A SUDDEN ATTACK

EXPLORE MORE

DURING THE MEXICAN-AMERICAN WAR, THE MARINES CAPTURED A CASTLE KNOWN AS THE HALLS OF MONTEZUMA. THE "MARINES' HYMN" REMEMBERS THAT VICTORY AND THE BATTLE OF DERNA: "FROM THE HALLS OF MONTEZUMA, TO THE SHORES OF TRIPOLI, WE FIGHT OUR COUNTRY'S BATTLES IN THE AIR, ON LAND, AND SEA."

THE UNITED STATES MARINE BAND IS OFTEN REFERRED TO AS "THE PRESIDENT'S OWN." PART OF THE BAND'S MISSION IS TO PERFORM FOR THE PRESIDENT.

Toward the end of World War II, a U.S. Marine Corps patrol had been given orders to capture the island of Iwo Jima, off the coast of Japan. The highest point on this small island was Mount Suribachi. Gaining control of the peak could help the marines capture the entire island.

On February 23, 1945, the patrol reached the top of Mount Suribachi and raised the U.S. flag, marking the capture. A photographer named Joe Rosenthal was at the summit when a group of marines raised a second, larger flag that would be easier to see from below. As the marines put up this flag, Rosenthal snapped a picture.

The image Rosenthal captured that day became the most famous photograph of World War II and is still one of the most famous photographs in the world. Although the Battle of Iwo Jima lasted for nearly another month, Rosenthal's photograph became a symbol of victory and courage, showing the power of the U.S. military, and specifically, the U.S. Marine Corps.

THE MARINE CORPS MEMORIAL IN ARLINGTON, VIRGINIA, WAS MODELED AFTER ROSENTHAL'S FAMOUS PHOTOGRAPH.

More than 75 years after the Battle of Iwo Jima, the corps still considers the fighting spirit of each U.S. Marine to be one of its greatest **assets**. Marines are trained to work through any kind of situation and keep fighting until they've reached victory. The main values of the marines are honor, courage, and commitment. Marines must be ready to step into battle at any moment and bring with them their strong spirit and **determination** to win.

Today, new marines, called recruits, go through a 13-week training process called boot camp. Here, they learn the values of the marine corps, as well as important skills. Boot camp is tough both physically and mentally.

Becoming an officer in the marines requires a college degree and training at Officer Candidates School. After that, new officers go to Basic School for further training and education. Then, they receive more specialized training in their chosen field. Only after all this will an officer be given command of other marines.

ROSENTHAL'S PHOTOGRAPH OF THE FLAG RAISING ON IWO JIMA WON HIM A PULITZER PRIZE IN 1945.

RELATIONSHIP WITH THE NAVY

The Marine Corps and the navy are two different forces in the U.S. military, but both work under the U.S. Department of the Navy. The marines and the navy have a close relationship that dates back to the beginning of the corps when the two groups worked together during the American Revolution. This was before the United States was even officially its own country. Today, many marine units work on U.S. Navy ships all over the world. This makes it much easier for marines to enter combat quickly when they are needed.

DEPLOY: TO MOVE TROOPS INTO A POSITION OF READINESS

MARINE UNITS ARE OFTEN DEPLOYED TO NAVAL WARSHIPS LIKE THE USS *HARPERS FERRY*.

CHAPTER TWO: MARINES AT WAR

The U.S. Marine Corps has a reputation for being a strong and fierce force. The service gained this reputation through many victories at war.

★ EXPLORE MORE ★

THE MARITIME PREPOSITIONING FORCE IS MADE UP OF SHIPS STATIONED AROUND THE WORLD. THEY CONTAIN ALL THE SUPPLIES THAT MARINES WOULD NEED FOR 30 DAYS OF COMBAT. THIS ALLOWS THE MARINES TO BEGIN OPERATING IN FARAWAY COUNTRIES AS QUICKLY AS POSSIBLE.

THE BATTLE OF BELLEAU WOOD HAPPENED IN JUNE 1918. AFTER NEARLY A MONTH OF FIGHTING, THE MARINES FORCED GERMAN TROOPS TO RETREAT.

In World War I, the marines became known for being tough and fearless fighters. Despite being outnumbered, they won the Battle of Belleau Wood in France. They earned the nickname "Devil Dogs," a name still used today.

In World War II, the Marine Corps played a major role in defeating the Japanese. Dozens of islands in the Pacific Ocean were controlled by Japanese forces. It was the marines' job to get control of the islands. To get ashore from the naval ships, the marines used small **vehicles** that could travel on both water and land. This tactic is called **amphibious** assault.

During World War II, the United States captured key islands in the Pacific Ocean, one by one. Eventually, U.S. bombers were able to reach Japan by flying from one island to another, which became known as island hopping. It was the job of the Marine Corps to capture these islands.

During the Korean War, the marines were called upon to recover South Korea's capital city of Seoul from the North Koreans. In what's known as the Inchon Landing, the marines used an amphibious assault to quickly land behind enemy lines and make their way toward Seoul. After two weeks, the North Korean army fled the city.

TACTIC: A METHOD FOR ACCOMPLISHING A MILITARY GOAL

GRENADE: A SMALL BOMB THROWN BY HAND OR USING A LAUNCHER

THE MEDAL OF HONOR

The highest award given to any member of the armed forces is called the Medal of Honor. The medal is given out by the U.S. government to honor the bravest military members. It was established in 1861 to honor members of the U.S. Navy. Today, it can be awarded to any member of the armed forces. Many marines have earned the honor, including First Lieutenant Baldomero Lopez. He died during the Inchon Landing when he bravely used his body to cover a grenade, protecting the lives of his fellow marines around him.

THIS PHOTOGRAPH SHOWS LOPEZ LEADING MARINES OVER A SEAWALL DURING THE INCHON LANDING.

In 1989, marines took part in a mission to capture Panamanian **dictator** Manuel Noriega who surrendered in Panama City on January 3, 1990.

EXPLORE MORE

IN 1991, THE MARINES TOOK PART IN A MILITARY OPERATION CALLED OPERATION DESERT STORM. THE GOAL WAS TO REMOVE IRAQI FORCES THAT HAD INVADED KUWAIT. MARINE PILOTS HELPED DESTROY IRAQ'S AIR AND NAVAL FORCES DURING THE OPERATION.

OPERATION DESERT STORM WAS PART OF WHAT'S NOW KNOWN AS THE PERSIAN GULF WAR (1990-1991).

On September 11, 2001, **terrorists** attacked New York City and Washington, DC. These events sparked what became known as the war on terrorism. The marines were deployed to the country of Afghanistan in an effort to beat al-Qaeda and Taliban forces. On November 25, 2001, the 15th Marine Expeditionary Unit (MEU) was the first of the U.S. ground troops to arrive in Afghanistan. They quickly seized an important airstrip. The Afghanistan War was the longest conflict the United States ever fought.

WHEN THE 15TH MARINE EXPEDITIONARY UNIT GOT TO AFGHANISTAN, THEY SET UP AN IMPORTANT BASE KNOWN AS CAMP RHINO.

COMPUTER CAMOUFLAGE

In 2002, the Marine Corps began using a new kind of computer-generated camouflage. Older kinds of camouflage used larger splotches of color. The newer camouflage is made up of overlapping squares that make it hard to detect, even with hi-tech cameras and tools. It looks a bit like **pixelated** images you might see in computer games. Tests have shown that this type of camouflage, called Marine pattern camouflage, or MARPAT, takes longer to be spotted than older styles of camouflage. Since the marines started using it, other U.S. military forces have started using similar patterns.

BLENDING IN

THIS IMAGE SHOWS WHAT MARPAT (CENTER) LOOKS LIKE IN A WOODED AREA COMPARED TO A PLAIN GREEN UNIFORM AND AN OLDER CAMOUFLAGE PATTERN. AS YOU CAN SEE, MARPAT BLENDS IN THE BEST.

Through history, the U.S. Marine Corps has shown its power during times of conflict. However, the corps doesn't just use its strength for combat. It also helps people during **natural disasters**, such as hurricanes. Certain units practice contingency plans to make sure they're ready to help when these disasters strike.

CONTINGENCY: AN EVENT, SUCH AS AN EMERGENCY, THAT MAY HAPPEN BUT ISN'T CERTAIN TO HAPPEN

CHAPTER THREE: GEAR UP

From simple knives to state-of-the-art fighter jets, the Marine Corps deals with many different kinds of weapons. For many marines, the most important weapon is their rifle. For many years, the M16 was the standard rifle used by the U.S. military. Marines had been using **versions** of the weapon since the mid-1960s. In 2003, the Marines started using an updated model called the M16A4.

In 2015, the U.S. Marine Corps switched to a new standard service rifle—the M4 Carbine. This is a lighter, smaller version of the M16. The M4 is said to be easier to handle and makes it easier for users to accurately shoot at faraway targets.

CARBINE: A SHORT, LIGHTWEIGHT RIFLE

★ EXPLORE MORE ★

AN IMPORTANT PART OF BEING A MARINE IS KNOWING HOW TO PROPERLY USE YOUR WEAPONS. ONE OF THE FIRST THINGS A MARINE IS TRAINED IN IS HOW TO HANDLE THEIR RIFLE.

In 2018, the Marine Corps replaced many M4s with a newer weapon, the M27 Infantry Automatic Rifle. It has provided for even better accuracy than the M4 and fires shots faster. The M4 is still used for some operations.

AN M27 CAN SHOOT ABOUT 330 TO 500 FEET (100 TO 152 M) FARTHER THAN AN M4.

REACHING THE RANKS

Marine ranks are divided into three categories: commissioned officer, warrant officer, and enlisted soldier. The enlisted ranks make up the majority of the corps. An enlisted marine who reaches the rank of corporal is considered a noncommissioned officer. Commissioned officers receive a formal document, or commission, from the president that gives them their rank and leadership duties. At first, warrant officers are noncommissioned officers who are experts in a certain field or with certain weapons. When someone reaches the rank of Chief Warrant Officer 2, they become a commissioned officer. To become a warrant officer, a marine must achieve the rank of sergeant.

ENLISTED: REFERRING TO MEMBERS OF THE MILITARY WHO RANK BELOW COMMISSIONED OR WARRANT OFFICERS

MARINE RANKS

COMMISSIONED OFFICERS:

- GENERAL
- LIEUTENANT GENERAL
- MAJOR GENERAL
- BRIGADIER GENERAL
- COLONEL
- LIEUTENANT COLONEL
- MAJOR
- CAPTAIN
- FIRST LIEUTENANT
- SECOND LIEUTENANT

WARRANT OFFICERS:

- CHIEF WARRANT OFFICER 5
- CHIEF WARRANT OFFICER 4
- CHIEF WARRANT OFFICER 3
- CHIEF WARRANT OFFICER 2
- WARRANT OFFICER

ENLISTED:

- SERGEANT MAJOR OF THE MARINE CORPS
- SERGEANT MAJOR
- MASTER GUNNERY SERGEANT
- FIRST SERGEANT
- MASTER SERGEANT
- GUNNERY SERGEANT
- STAFF SERGEANT
- SERGEANT
- CORPORAL
- LANCE CORPORAL
- PRIVATE FIRST CLASS
- PRIVATE

THIS CHART SHOWS THE DIFFERENT RANKS A MARINE CAN HOLD. THE POSITIONS IN EACH GROUP ARE LISTED FROM HIGHEST RANK TO LOWEST RANK.

M1A1 ABRAMS TANKS ARE USED TO FIRE AT ENEMY TARGETS AND CARRY MARINES.

When you think of military weapons, you may think mainly of guns, but vehicles are also important weapons. Marines use a variety of vehicles, such as the M1A1 Abrams tank. The marines are continuously using the latest technology to update these advanced tanks commonly used in battle.

An amphibious assault vehicle (AAV) is an armored vehicle made to carry marines on land and water. AAVs are commonly used to carry troops from a ship to land during combat. Once they reach land, these vehicles can keep moving, protecting troops from enemy fire. These tanks are also armed, so troops use them to fight as well. The U.S. Marine Corps has built the most advanced AAVs.

★ EXPLORE MORE ★

THE HIGGINS BOAT WAS ONE OF THE MARINE CORPS' EARLIEST AMPHIBIOUS VEHICLES. INVENTED BY ANDREW HIGGINS, IT WAS WIDELY USED DURING WORLD WAR II TO CARRY TROOPS AND SUPPLIES FROM SHIP TO SHORE.

In late 2019, the Marine Corps tested a new vehicle, the Amphibious Combat Vehicle (ACV). While similar to AAVs, ACVs are even more advanced and are created to be able to better handle missions involving bringing troops from ships to shore. As more testing is completed, the marines plan to replace AAVs with ACVs.

The marines also use aircraft to support ground forces during missions. Perhaps the most famous is the jet called the AV-8B Harrier. The marines have been using these powerful aircraft for more than 30 years. Still an important vehicle for the force after all these years, Harriers can take off straight up and hover in midair. This allows the Harrier to be used in places without a runway.

HARRIERS WERE THE FIRST TACTICAL AIRCRAFT OF THE U.S. MARINES TO GET TO OPERATION DESERT STORM.

HI-TECH HELICOPTERS

Helicopters are important aircraft for the marines. Like Harriers, helicopters are built to be able to hover in the air. Spinning blades on top, called the rotor, allow helicopters to fly. The AH-1Z Viper is a powerful attack helicopter used by the U.S. Marine Corps. These helicopters provide reconnaissance from the air. They also attack from the air, providing support to forces on the ground. The advanced technology of the Viper allows the marines to detect and respond to threats along the route of the flight. The vehicle can also scan landing zones to make sure they're safe before touching down.

RECONNAISSANCE: THE EXPLORATION OF A PLACE TO COLLECT INFORMATION

THE MARINE CORPS PROVIDES HELICOPTER TRANSPORTATION FOR THE PRESIDENT OF THE UNITED STATES. WHEN THE PRESIDENT IS ONBOARD A MARINE CORPS HELICOPTER, IT'S CALLED MARINE ONE.

CHAPTER FOUR: FAMOUS MARINES

Some marines have become famous for their heroic actions during service. Others served in the marines before becoming famous for other reasons.

Many American astronauts were marines first. One of the best known among these marines is John Glenn. Glenn served as a fighter pilot in World War II and Korea. In 1962, he became the first American to orbit Earth. In 1998, he went to space again. This time, he was 77 years old, becoming the oldest person to ever go to space.

GLENN, WHO DIED IN 2016, FLEW 59 COMBAT MISSIONS DURING WORLD WAR II. DURING THE KOREAN WAR, HE FLEW 63 MORE MISSIONS.

WOMEN IN THE MARINES

Women have held official positions within the U.S. Marine Corps since 1918. On August 13 of that year, Opha May Jacob Johnson became the first woman to enlist in the marine corps. Around 300 other women also joined the marines that year. These women served mainly in administrative positions. In 1942, the Marine Corps Women's Reserve was created. Women in the reserve performed more than 200 different kinds of jobs, from radio operator to parachute rigger. Many of these roles had previously been held by men who were sent into combat during World War II. As of 2020, women made up about 8 percent of the U.S. Marine Corps.

Throughout history, many Native American tribes have used their languages as codes to help the U.S. military. During World War II, young marines who were Diné, or Navajo, used their language to create a secret code to send messages. The language didn't have a written alphabet, so enemies couldn't get their hands on any material that could help them decode it. The method was fast and secure—and impossible for the Japanese to decode. By the time the war ended, about 400 Navajo had served throughout all divisions of the U.S. Marine Corps. Now called the Navajo Code Talkers, these men did work that saved many lives.

★ EXPLORE MORE ★

THE MARINE CORPS' MOTTO IS *SEMPER FIDELIS*. THESE LATIN WORDS MEAN "ALWAYS FAITHFUL." OFTEN SHORTENED TO SEMPER FI, IT REMINDS MARINES TO BE FAITHFUL TO THE MISSION, EACH OTHER, THE CORPS, AND THE COUNTRY.

MILITARY PHONETIC ALPHABET

A: ALPHA
B: BRAVO
C: CHARLIE
D: DELTA
E: ECHO
F: FOXTROT
G: GOLF
H: HOTEL
I: INDIA
J: JULIET
K: KILO
L: LIMA
M: MIKE
N: NOVEMBER
O: OSCAR
P: PAPA
Q: QUEBEC
R: ROMEO
S: SIERRA
T: TANGO
U: UNIFORM
V: VICTOR
W: WHISKEY
X: XRAY
Y: YANKEE
Z: ZULU

WHEN SPEAKING OVER THE RADIO, MEMBERS OF THE MILITARY USE WORDS TO REPRESENT LETTERS. THIS IS CALLED THE PHONETIC ALPHABET. IT HELPS AVOID CONFUSION AND MISUNDERSTANDINGS OF WORDS.

Several celebrities served in the marines. Drew Carey, host of *The Price Is Right*, was in the Marines Corps Reserve. Rob Riggle, who's been in movies and TV shows such as *Saturday Night Live*, *Hotel Transylvania*, and *Modern Family*, was in the marines for more than 20 years.

RESERVE: REFERRING TO SOLDIERS WHO ARE NOT PART OF A COUNTRY'S MAIN FORCES, BUT MAY BE CALLED TO ACTIVE DUTY IN TIMES OF NEED

Perhaps the most famous former marine working in Hollywood today is Adam Driver. Driver is known for his many acting roles, most notably Kylo Ren in several *Star Wars* movies. But before he was a star on screen, Driver was a marine. He's said the attacks on September 11, 2001, made him want to enlist. He was planning to deploy when he got hurt in a mountain-biking accident.

AFTER TWO YEARS OF SERVICE, DRIVER WAS HONORABLY DISCHARGED FROM THE MARINES FOR MEDICAL REASONS.

AMMUNITION: BULLETS, SHELLS, AND OTHER THINGS FIRED BY WEAPONS

SHRAPNEL: SMALL PIECES FROM AN EXPLODING WEAPON

CORPS CREATURES

Believe it or not, not all the workers in the marines are human! Animals play a key role in the corps too! Military working dogs are often used in areas of conflict to sniff out explosives and guard their human counterparts. Even a horse has served in the marines! During the Korean War (1950–1953), a horse named Sergeant Reckless carried ammunition to troops, usually without a human guiding her. She also carried hurt marines to safety and kept working even after she had been hit by shrapnel. Sergeant Reckless was the only animal in the marines to ever be given an official rank.

MARINE BOOT CAMP IS HELD AT THE MARINE CORPS RECRUIT DEPOT IN PARRIS ISLAND, SOUTH CAROLINA, OR SAN DIEGO, CALIFORNIA.

★ EXPLORE MORE ★

MARINE CORPS BOOT CAMP IS CONSIDERED ONE OF THE TOUGHEST IN THE WORLD. RECRUITS LEARN HOW TO ACT QUICKLY AND MAKE THE RIGHT DECISIONS WITHOUT SECOND-GUESSING THEMSELVES.

From the moment they start boot camp, marines are faced with serious challenges they must learn to work through. Whether working stateside as a member of the reserve or across the world on a naval ship, every marine's job is important. From combat missions to helping people during natural disasters, the U.S. Marine Corps is always ready to respond on land, on water, and in the air.

HURRICANE MARIA WAS A DESTRUCTIVE HURRICANE IN THE CARIBBEAN IN 2017. AFTER THE STORM, MANY MARINES WENT TO PUERTO RICO TO HELP WITH RELIEF EFFORTS.

GLOSSARY

amphibious Having the ability to operate on both land and water.

asset A valuable person or thing.

determination The act of deciding something firmly.

dictator Someone who rules a country by force.

front An area where a military force is fighting.

natural disaster A severe event in nature that commonly results in serious damage and deaths.

pixelated Made up of a number of large pixels, or parts, that produce an unclear picture.

terrorist One who uses violence and fear to challenge an authority.

vehicle An object used for carrying or transporting people or goods, such as a car, truck, or airplane.

version A form of something that is different from others.

FOR MORE INFORMATION

BOOKS

Jones, Keisha. *My Brother Is in the Marine Corps*. New York, NY: PowerKids Press, 2016.

London, C. Alexander. *Tides of War: Honor Bound*. New York, NY: Scholastic Inc., 2014.

Slater, Lee. *Marine Force Recon*. Minneapolis, MN: Abdo Publishing, 2016.

Sutter, Marcus. *Secret Mission: Guam*. New York, NY: HarperFestival, 2019.

WEBSITES

Birth of the U.S. Marine Corps
www.history.com/this-day-in-history/birth-of-the-u-s-marine-corps
Check out this website to read more about the beginning of the U.S. Marine Corps.

Marines
www.marines.mil/
Find out all about the Marines and keep up with the latest news on the branch's official website.

National Museum of the Marine Corps
www.usmcmuseum.com/
Learn more about the Marine Corps and look at exhibits on the National Museum of the Marine Corps's website.

Publisher's note to educators and parents: Our editors have carefully reviewed these websites to ensure that they are suitable for students. Many websites change frequently, however, and we cannot guarantee that a site's future contents will continue to meet our high standards of quality and educational value. Be advised that students should be closely supervised whenever they access the internet.

INDEX